TPM Tag Register

Project Date: ____________________ Work Area: ____________________

Item Description	Date Sorted	Log Number	Reason for Tag	Classification (i.e. need approval, other dept. needs to assess, throw out, etc.)

A **Productivity Press** Product

www.enna.com
www.productivitypress.com

TPM Tag Register

Project Date: ____________________ Work Area: ____________________

Item Description	Date Sorted	Log Number	Reason for Tag	Classification (i.e. need approval, other dept. needs to assess, throw out, etc.)

TPM Tag Register

Project Date: ____________________ Work Area: ____________________

Item Description	Date Sorted	Log Number	Reason for Tag	Classification (i.e. need approval, other dept. needs to assess, throw out, etc.)

TPM Tag Register

Project Date: ____________________ Work Area: ____________________

Item Description	Date Sorted	Log Number	Reason for Tag	Classification (I.e. need approval, other dept. needs to assess, throw out, etc.)

TPM Tag Register

Project Date: ____________________ Work Area: ____________________

Item Description	Date Sorted	Log Number	Reason for Tag	Classification (I.e. need approval, other dept. needs to assess, throw out, etc.)

TPM Tag Register

Project Date: ____________________ Work Area: ____________________

Item Description	Date Sorted	Log Number	Reason for Tag	Classification (i.e. need approval, other dept. needs to assess, throw out, etc.)

TPM Tag Register

Project Date: ____________________ Work Area: ____________________

Item Description	Date Sorted	Log Number	Reason for Tag	Classification (i.e. need approval, other dept. needs to assess, throw out, etc.)

TPM Tag Register

Project Date: ____________________ Work Area: ____________________

Item Description	Date Sorted	Log Number	Reason for Tag	Classification (i.e. need approval, other dept. needs to assess, throw out, etc.)

TPM Tag Register

Project Date: ____________________ Work Area: ____________________

Item Description	Date Sorted	Log Number	Reason for Tag	Classification (i.e. need approval, other dept. needs to assess, throw out, etc.)

TPM Tag Register

Project Date: ____________________ Work Area: ____________________

Item Description	Date Sorted	Log Number	Reason for Tag	Classification (i.e. need approval, other dept. needs to assess, throw out, etc.)

A **Productivity Press** Product

www.enna.com
www.productivitypress.com

TPM Tag Register

Project Date: ______________________ Work Area: ______________________

Item Description	Date Sorted	Log Number	Reason for Tag	Classification (i.e. need approval, other dept. needs to assess, throw out, etc.)

TPM Tag Register

Project Date: ____________________ Work Area: ____________________

Item Description	Date Sorted	Log Number	Reason for Tag	Classification (i.e. need approval, other dept. needs to assess, throw out, etc.)

TPM Tag Register

Project Date: ______________________ Work Area: ______________________

Item Description	Date Sorted	Log Number	Reason for Tag	Classification (i.e. need approval, other dept. needs to assess, throw out, etc.)

TPM Tag Register

Project Date: ____________________ Work Area: ____________________

Item Description	Date Sorted	Log Number	Reason for Tag	Classification (i.e. need approval, other dept. needs to assess, throw out, etc.)

TPM Tag Register

Project Date: ____________________ Work Area: ____________________

Item Description	Date Sorted	Log Number	Reason for Tag	Classification (I.e. need approval, other dept. needs to assess, throw out, etc.)

A **Productivity Press** Product

www.enna.com
www.productivitypress.com

TPM Tag Register

Project Date: ____________________ Work Area: ____________________

Item Description	Date Sorted	Log Number	Reason for Tag	Classification (i.e. need approval, other dept. needs to assess, throw out, etc.)

TPM Tag Register

Project Date: ____________________ Work Area: ____________________

Item Description	Date Sorted	Log Number	Reason for Tag	Classification (i.e. need approval, other dept. needs to assess, throw out, etc.)

TPM Tag Register

Project Date: ____________________ Work Area: ____________________

Item Description	Date Sorted	Log Number	Reason for Tag	Classification (i.e. need approval, other dept. needs to assess, throw out, etc.)

A **Productivity Press** Product

www.enna.com
www.productivitypress.com

TPM Tag Register

Project Date: ____________________ Work Area: ____________________

Item Description	Date Sorted	Log Number	Reason for Tag	Classification (i.e. need approval, other dept. needs to assess, throw out, etc.)

TPM Tag Register

Project Date: ____________________ Work Area: ____________________

Item Description	Date Sorted	Log Number	Reason for Tag	Classification (i.e. need approval, other dept. needs to assess, throw out, etc.)

TPM Tag Register

Project Date: ____________________ Work Area: ____________________

Item Description	Date Sorted	Log Number	Reason for Tag	Classification (i.e. need approval, other dept. needs to assess, throw out, etc.)

TPM Tag Register

Project Date: ____________________ Work Area: ____________________

Item Description	Date Sorted	Log Number	Reason for Tag	Classification (I.e. need approval, other dept. needs to assess, throw out, etc.)

TPM Tag Register

Project Date: ____________________ Work Area: ____________________

Item Description	Date Sorted	Log Number	Reason for Tag	Classification (i.e. need approval, other dept. needs to assess, throw out, etc.)

TPM Tag Register

Project Date: ____________________ Work Area: ____________________

Item Description	Date Sorted	Log Number	Reason for Tag	Classification (i.e. need approval, other dept. needs to assess, throw out, etc.)

TPM Tag Register

Project Date: ______________________

Work Area: ______________________

Item Description	Date Sorted	Log Number	Reason for Tag	Classification (i.e. need approval, other dept. needs to assess, throw out, etc.)